SCIENCE WORLD

FORCES
IN ACTION

KATHRYN WHYMAN

Franklin Watts
London • Sydney

© Archon Press 2003

Produced by
Archon Press Ltd
28 Percy Street
London W1T 2BZ

New edition first published in
Great Britain in 2003 by
Franklin Watts
96 Leonard Street
London EC2A 4XD

Original edition published as
Simply Science – Forces in Action

ISBN 0-7496-5108-3

Designer:
Pete Bennett – PBD

Editor:
Katie Harker

Picture Researcher:
Brian Hunter Smart

Illustrator:
Louise Nevett

Printed in UAE

531 6

CONTENTS

INTRODUCTION

Forces change the way things move. They make an object move slower or faster or they can change an object's direction or shape. You can't see a force – you can only see or feel its effect.

You exert forces yourself all the time, whenever you pick up a pen, open a book or walk along a street. And forces are exerted on you, too. When the wind blows on your face, or you stop suddenly in a car, or a book falls on your foot, you can feel the effects of forces acting on you.

Fairground rides produce a number of forces that spin you around or turn you upside down.

In this book you will find out about different forces and the effect that they can have on you, as well as objects around you – from the natural pull of gravity and the strength of the wind, to the work of machinery. You will also discover how simple machines help us to overcome forces. Knowing about forces will help you to understand why things move in the way they do.

Windsurfers use the force of the wind to carry them across the water.

NATURAL FORCES

Forces occur naturally in a number of forms. Forces can cause harm but they can also be useful. The wind exerts a force which can blow down a tree or damage buildings. But the wind can also be used to move sailing boats, generate electricity or even to fly flags and kites.

The tremendous force of waves on a stormy day can make conditions very dangerous for boats, and a flowing river can cause damaging floods. But rivers can also be used to carry timber downstream, or turn a water wheel.

Gravity, too, is a natural force. You will find out more about gravity later in this book (see page 20).

In some places, tornadoes (violent whirlwinds) are a frequent threat to property and dwellings.

The force of the waves can be both useful and harmful to boats and other sailing vessels.

Windmills use the force of the wind to pump water, grind corn or to generate electricity.

MAKING FORCES

Although forces occur naturally, they can also be produced by people or machines. Often these forces are comprised of pushes, pulls or twists. You probably use forces like these every day – like when you push a door bell, open a drawer or twist a bottle top.

We also use machines to produce forces on our behalf. Machines can be made to exert a greater force than we can produce ourselves. For example, a tractor can pull a trailer full of hay, a bulldozer can push forward a mound of earth and a potter's wheel turns and helps to shape a vase out of a lump of clay. Look around you and you will see many forces in action.

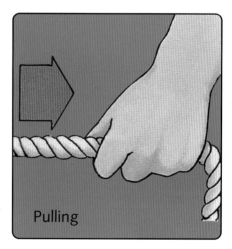

Pulling

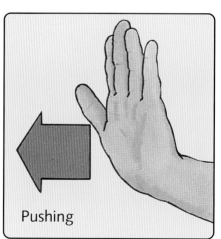

Pushing

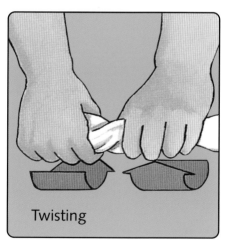

Twisting

You can exert a force by pulling. Pulling a rope attached to a sledge will make the sledge move forwards. You use many pulling forces every day – like doing up a zip, pulling the curtains, putting socks on and pulling a door closed.

Sometimes you exert a force by pushing – you can push a table across a room, push a swing door to open it, push a trolley or push a parcel through a letter box. When you push and pull you use your weight to exert a force onto an object.

You can also exert a number of forces by twisting – you might wring out wet clothes to dry them, turn a wheel, open a jam jar, turn a screwdriver or wind up a clock. Twisting forces are usually conducted with your arms and your hands.

These rowers use a pulling action to propel their boat through the water.

A bulldozer pushing forward a mound of earth

Electric drills use a twisting force.

WHAT CAN FORCES DO?

Forces change the way things move. The force of the wind will alter the direction of a hot air balloon. Meanwhile, a moving ball, with no forces acting on it, will continue moving in the same direction and at the same speed until a force acts upon it.

A force can also change the shape of an object. A giant crusher can change the shape of a car – even your hand can exert a force to shape and mould certain objects.

Whenever we find that the speed or direction of a moving object is changing, or the shape is changing, we say that forces are acting to cause these changes.

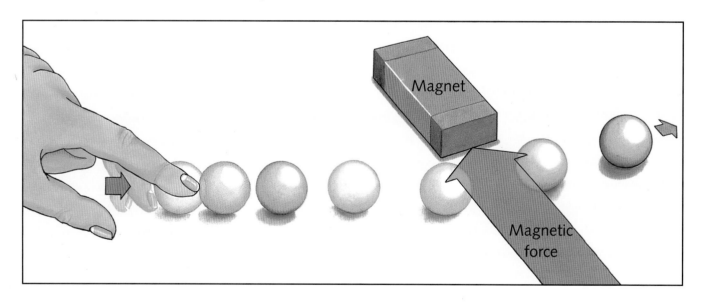

The diagram above illustrates the force exerted on a steel ball by the flick of a finger. We can see that the force sets the ball moving, and when the force stops, the ball continues in a straight line at a constant speed, unless another force acts on it. When a magnet is held near the moving ball, it exerts a pulling force on it – changing the direction of the ball. This is because magnets attract steel.

Right: The force of the wind can increase the speed of a yacht as it catches in the sails.

FORCES AT WORK

A force can change the shape of an object and the greater the force, the greater the change it brings about. Although you can dent a wall with a hammer, a metal ball could knock a whole building down.

When you lift yourself up onto a wall you push down on the top of the wall with your hands. As you push, you exert a force which acts downwards on the wall, and the wall pushes against your hands, lifting you upwards. This force is equal to the force exerted by your hands, but it acts in the opposite direction. Gymnasts use a similar action to perform. Opposite forces in action can also be seen when a rocket takes off (right).

Large push, pull and twisting forces are required to demolish a building.

Burning gases push downwards when a rocket is launched, forcing the rocket upwards.

FRICTION

When two objects rub against each other they cause 'friction'. Friction is vitally important in our lives. Friction between our shoes and the ground stops us from slipping over when we walk. Friction between tyres and the road allows cars and lorries to move forwards and prevents them from skidding. Friction also causes heat – you can start a fire by rubbing two sticks together.

Friction also slows things down. A ball rolling along the ground will gradually get slower until it stops, because of friction between the ball and the ground. Car and bicycle brakes also use friction to slow a moving vehicle down.

Bicycle brakes

When blocks of rubber squeeze against the sides of a bicycle wheel, friction stops the wheel from turning. But the bicycle itself will only stop if there is enough friction between the tyres and the road – brakes are of little use in icy conditions.

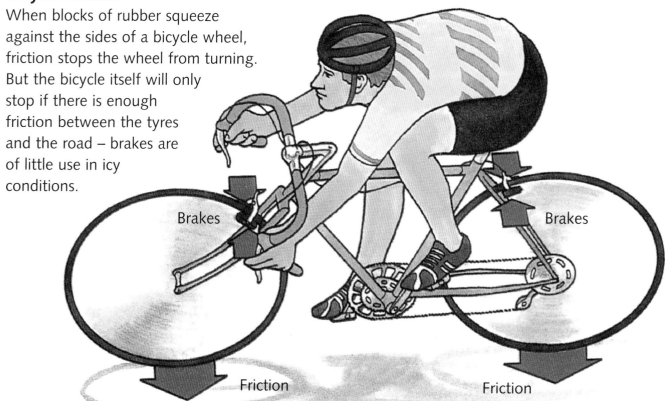

Brakes

Brakes

Friction

Friction

Friction between your shoes and the ground stops you from slipping over when you run (top). A rolling ball will eventually stop because of friction between the ball and the ground (top right). You can produce enough heat to start a fire by rubbing two sticks together (right). Friction between tyres and the track stops motorbikes from skidding (below).

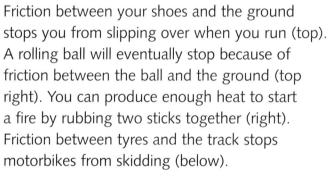

REDUCING FRICTION

Friction makes it difficult to rub two dry, rough surfaces together. The thin blades of ice skates move easily on ice because there is little friction between the two smooth surfaces. Sometimes, friction can be used to make a surface smoother. For example, sandpaper is rubbed over wood to wear away the rough edges.

Friction can also wear away moving parts in a machine, eventually ruining them. To prevent this, a lubricant, such as oil, is used. Oiled door hinges will move against each other easily and there will be little wear. Some machines, like aeroplanes and cars, are also designed to reduce friction between the body and surrounding air particles.

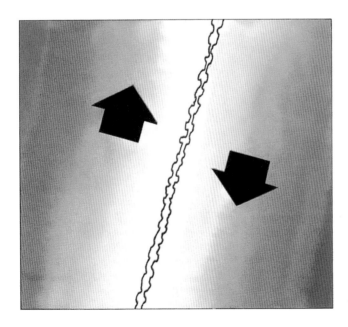

If you magnify two surfaces which look smooth you can see that they are actually quite rough. As you rub the surfaces together they scrape against each other. Friction slows down their movement and wears them away.

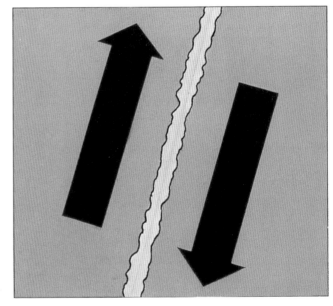

Putting oil between surfaces (like the parts in a car engine) helps to make them smooth and wet. The materials can now be moved quickly and easily against each other, which reduces friction, and prevents the surfaces from being worn away.

The thin blades on ice hockey boots move easily on the wet, smooth surface of ice.

Sports cars have a streamlined design to reduce friction between the moving vehicle and air particles.

ELASTIC FORCES

We have seen that forces can change the shape of things. But sometimes the changes are not always permanent. A rubber band will stretch, but as soon as you let go it will return to its original shape. As it does so, it exerts a force – called an 'elastic force'.

Metals are harder to stretch but they can exert a greater elastic force. Metals are often coiled to make springs – to be used for machinery parts or trampolines, or to make seats and mattresses more comfortable for example.

Elastic forces are also used to absorb a large force – like breaking the fall of a bungee jumper.

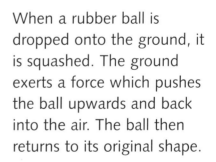

When a rubber ball is dropped onto the ground, it is squashed. The ground exerts a force which pushes the ball upwards and back into the air. The ball then returns to its original shape.

Elastic forces break the fall of this bungee jumper.

When an archer flexes his bow, the elastic force propels the arrow forward once it is released.

GRAVITY

If you jump in the air you will soon fall back down to the ground again. Snowboarders and skiers can jump high, but only for a moment. Sky-divers will also fall towards the Earth at a great speed. This is because the Earth has its own pulling forces called 'gravity'. The pull of gravity gradually becomes weaker as you move further away from the Earth's surface.

Like Earth, the Moon, the stars and other planets also have a gravitational pull of their own. Jupiter is much larger than the Earth so it has a stronger gravitational pull. The Moon is smaller than the Earth, so its force of gravity is weaker than the Earth's.

However high you jump, gravity will bring you and the ball back down to Earth again.

A man weighs six times less on the Moon than on Earth, because of the Moon's weaker gravity.

What is weight?

The weight of an object depends on how strong the gravitational pull is. The Earth's strong gravitational force pulls this boulder downwards, making it heavy and difficult to lift (below).

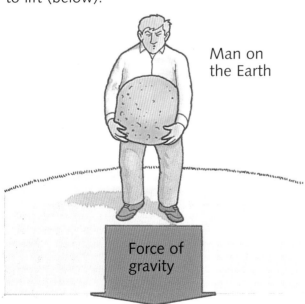

Man on the Earth

Force of gravity

Man on the Moon

Force of gravity

An astronaut would find the boulder easier to lift because the downwards pull of gravity on the Moon is less powerful than on Earth.

CENTRIPETAL FORCES

A moving object always travels in a straight line unless a force acts upon it. When a weight is spun round quickly on a string, it moves in a circle. This means that a force must be making the weight change its direction all the time. As the object spins you can feel the string pulling on your fingers. The string also pulls on the weight. It is this pull that makes the weight change its direction – a 'centripetal' force.

When you sit in a ride at a funfair, or in a car moving fast around a roundabout, you will also feel the effects of centripetal force. As the car turns, it pulls you with it, exerting centripetal force on you as it does so.

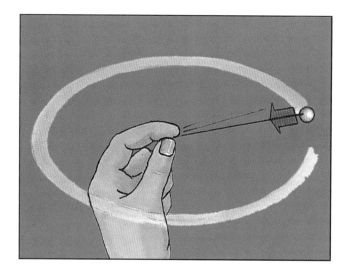
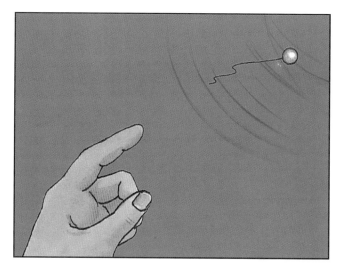

Going round in circles

As long as the weight is spinning fast enough, a centripetal force acts inwards to keep the weight moving in a circle. The force, shown by the arrow, acts along the line of the string.

Once the string is released there is no longer a centripetal force acting on the weight. With no force to keep the weight moving in a circle it flies off in a straight line, until another force acts upon it.

A satellite moves around the Moon in a circular path because of the centripetal force of gravity.

Centripetal forces keep this bobsleigh moving in a circle around the track.

OVERCOMING FORCES

'Weight' is the force exerted by gravity on a body. To lift something up, you must exert a greater upward force to overcome the downward force. The amount of 'work' you have to do to achieve this depends on the weight of the object and the distance you have to move it. Some things are too heavy for you to lift alone, and you need help – another person or a machine perhaps. Machines make our lives easier by doing work or helping us to do work.

A lever is a simple machine which can help you lift things, like the lid of a tin. Ramps can also overcome force – it is easier to roll an object than to lift it.

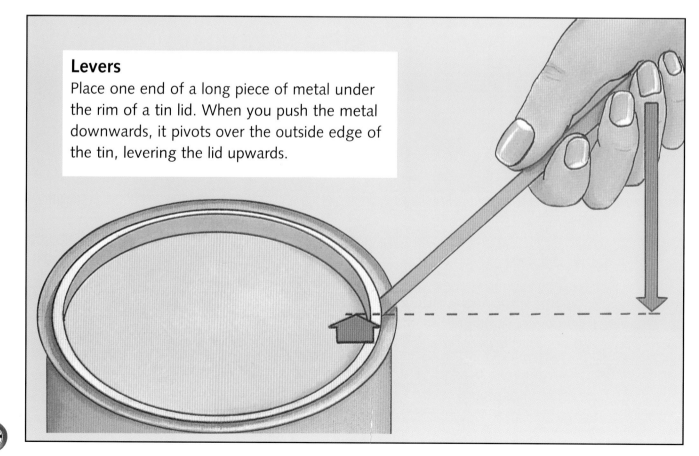

Levers
Place one end of a long piece of metal under the rim of a tin lid. When you push the metal downwards, it pivots over the outside edge of the tin, levering the lid upwards.

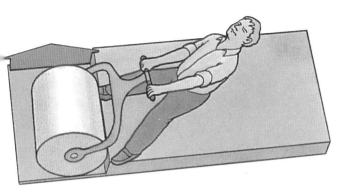
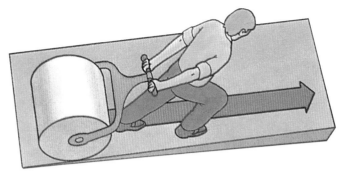

Ramps

A ramp is a type of simple machine used to help us lift heavy objects. The roller in the diagram above has to be raised 50 cm. It could be lifted up a step 50 cm high, but this would be very difficult to do (above left), because the roller is so heavy. By using a ramp (the top of which is the same height above the ground as the step – 50 cm), it is easier to pull the roller up the slope, even though the slope is long (above right).

This digger uses a combination of levers to scrape large amounts of earth from the ground.

PULLEYS AND GEARS

Pulleys are machines that we use to lift heavy objects. They are made from a number of wheels and a long piece of rope or cable. The cable is wound around each of the wheels in turn, and the whole system is attached to a weight.

By pulling the cable, the weight can be raised easily. The more wheels in a pulley system, the easier the lifting becomes. When three pulleys are used, the weight is shared between three stretches of cable and the force you need is only a third of what you would need to lift the weight by yourself. If four were used, the force you would need would be reduced to a quarter.

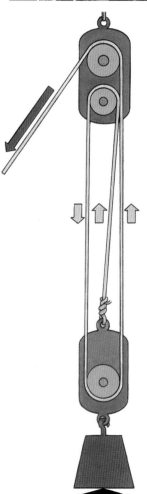

Cranes on a building site use pulleys to lift extremely heavy weights.

Cyclists use low gears to help them climb uphill.

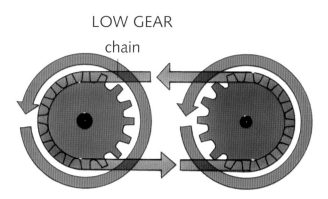

LOW GEAR
chain

Both wheels make one full turn.

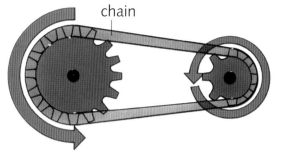

HIGH GEAR
chain

Pedal wheel makes one half turn.

Back wheel makes one full turn.

Gears

Like pulleys, gears make work easier. Gears are objects which are used to move force from one place to another. The most common gear is the cog – a wheel with teeth. In cars and bicycles, gears are used to help turn the wheels. On a bicycle, a chain moves around two cogs – a large cog attached to the pedals and a smaller cog attached to the back wheel.

As the pedals turn, the large cog rotates, the chain turns and the smaller cog makes the back wheel rotate quickly. If the large cog has twice as many teeth as the small cog, the back wheel will turn twice as quickly when you pedal. The smaller the cog at the rear, the faster you will travel (a high gear). The larger the cog at the rear, the lower the gear.

MAKE YOUR OWN MOUSETRAP

Make this mousetrap and see how ramps, levers, pushing, pulling and elastic forces all work in action. Although this trap won't catch any mice, it's fun to make! The instructions opposite will show you all you need to know.

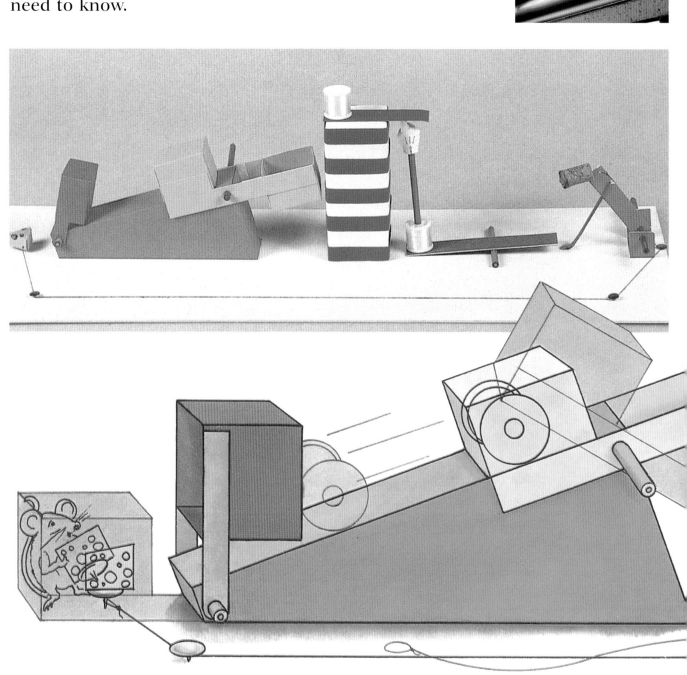

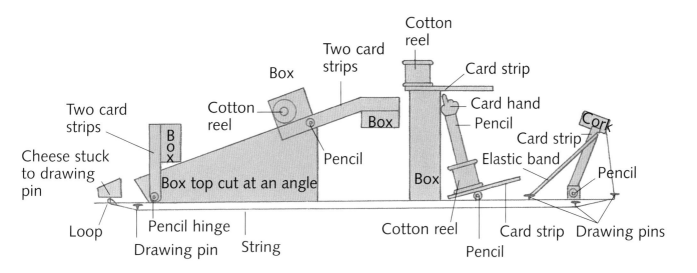

Cotton reel

Two card strips

Box

Card strip

Card hand

Two card strips

Cotton reel

Box

Pencil

Cork

Cheese stuck to drawing pin

B O X

Box

Card strip

Elastic band

Pencil

Box top cut at an angle

Pencil

Box

Loop

Pencil hinge

Cotton reel

Card strip

Drawing pins

Drawing pin

String

Pencil

Pencil

How to start

Cut the top of a cereal packet diagonally to make the sloping orange box.

The hinges

Make a hinge to attach the red box. Stick two strong pieces of card to either side of this small box and push a pencil through them and the orange box. All the other hinges can be made in this way.

Finishing the trap

Whatever you use to make the yellow boxes, they must be large enough to hold the cotton reels. The blue and white box must be the tallest one. Make sure the elastic band and the string are tightly stretched, and the cardboard cheese must be firmly attached to its drawing pin. When the cheese is removed, the trap is set in motion. Sit back and watch all the different forces at work!

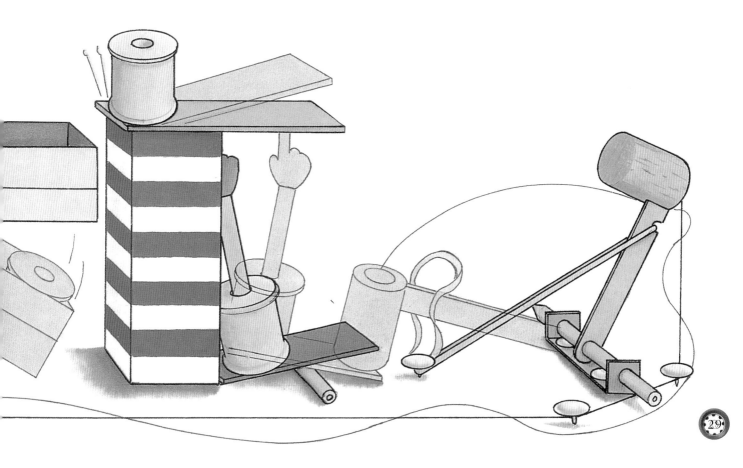

MORE ABOUT FORCES

Measuring forces

The size of a force depends on two things: the mass (amount of matter) of the object and its acceleration (see page 31). Imagine two vehicles driving along the road with the same acceleration. One is a lorry and the other is a small car. The lorry has the larger force because it has a greater mass than the car. Now imagine two identical cars with the same mass. They move slowly and then gradually speed up. But one of the cars gets faster more quickly than the other one and overtakes it. We say that this car has greater acceleration. The car with the higher acceleration has the greater force. Force is measured in units called NEWTONS.

Force = mass x acceleration

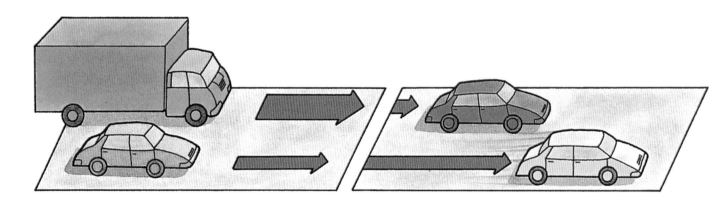

Measuring work

To raise an object you have to do work to it. The work you have to do depends on the force on the object you are lifting and the distance you are going to raise it. Work is measured in units called JOULES.

Work = force x distance

A box exerts a force of 50 newtons on the ground (right). You want to lift it onto a table 1 metre high. The amount of work you have to do is 50 joules.

50 newtons (force) x 1 metre (distance) = 50 joules (work)

GLOSSARY

Acceleration
A measurement of how quickly the speed of a moving object is increasing.

Brake
A device that slows the motion of a vehicle or a machine. A bicycle brake stops the wheel from turning.

Centripetal force
The inwards force that keeps a body moving in a curved path around a centre.

Cog
A toothed wheel.

Elastic
A material that regains its original size and shape after it has been squeezed or squashed is said to be elastic.

Friction
When two objects touch each other friction makes it difficult for them to move against each other. Friction can also cause heat.

Gears
A system of cogs which transfers movement from one part of a machine to another. Bicycle gears change the speed of the back wheel to help the cyclist to travel uphill.

Gravity
The invisible force exerted by the Sun, the Earth, the Moon or other planets in space. The Earth's gravity attracts objects, around the surface, towards the centre of the Earth.

Lever
A simple machine for lifting weights or for prising something open.

Lubricant
A substance, usually a liquid, such as oil, or grease which reduces friction when it is placed between two touching surfaces.

Machine
A device which enables the user to do a piece of work with less effort. For example, machines can help you to lift something heavy. Levers, pulleys and ramps are used in this way. Tools like spanners, screwdrivers and hammers are also examples of simple machines.

Magnet
A piece of iron or steel which exerts a special force called a 'magnetic' force. Magnets attract bits of iron or steel but repel the force of other magnets.

Mass
The amount of matter, or 'stuff', in an object. Mass is not the same as 'weight'. The mass of an object does not depend on the effect of a force like gravity which varies depending on where you are in the universe.

Pivot
A point about which a body turns freely. For example, when a lever is used to prise open a tin lid, it pivots over the edge of the tin.

Pulley
A simple machine made of wheels and a rope or cable, used for lifting heavy weights with a small amount of force.

Ramp
A simple machine used to lift heavy objects up a step.

Streamlined
The design of a body, such as a car, aircraft or ship, that helps it to move smoothly through air or water because it reduces friction.

Weight
The measurement of how heavy an object is. Weight varies depending on the force of gravity exerted on the object.

INDEX

Photocredits Abbreviations: l-left, r-right, b-bottom, t-top, c-centre, m-middle. Front cover main, back cover main, 1, 5b, 6tr, 8tr, 11, 12tr, 15tl, 16tr, 17t, 18bl, 19, 20b, 27 — Photodisc. Front cover mt, 2-3, 4tl, 6tl, 7b, 8tl, 10tl, 12tl, 14 both, 15b, 16tl, 18tl, 20tl, 20tr, 22tl, 24tl, 26tl, 26b, 28tl, 30t, 31t, 32t — Digital Stock. Front cover mb, 9bl, 25b — John Deere. 4tr, 4b, 5tr, 6b, 10tr, 13, 15tr, 15mr, 21t, 22tr, 23t, 24tr, 28tr — Corbis. 7t — NOAA Photo Library. 9t, 23b — Corel. 9br, 12b, 26tr — Select Pictures. 18tr — Ingram Publishing. 30br — Flat Earth.